Danny and the Time Train

by **Jillian Powell**

illustrated by **Alexa Rutherford**

Chapter One

The house where Danny lived had a long, thin garden. At the bottom of the garden was an old railway line. No trains had run there for over thirty years. Now, the tracks were old and rusty. Tall weeds and nettles grew over them.

Danny loved playing on the old railway line. Sometimes, he rode his bike between the tracks. Sometimes, he played football with old tin cans. He kicked them along the tracks, making them bounce and rattle.

It was a good place to explore. There was always something new to find, like a kite or an old bicycle wheel.

Chapter Two

One night, Danny couldn't sleep. He lay in bed, tossing and turning. He plumped up his pillow, but still he couldn't sleep.

Beep! went his clock. Ten o'clock. Beep! Eleven o'clock. Another beep, and Danny knew it must be midnight.

Then he heard a strange sound. It was a sort of chuff, chuff, chuffing sound. It reminded him of something, but before he could think what, he fell asleep.

The next night, the same thing happened. At exactly midnight, Danny heard the same sound. Chuff, chuff, chuff. It sounded just like a steam train, but that was impossible. No trains could run on the old railway line.

Danny had to find out what the sound was. On the third night, he went to bed in his tracksuit. He lay awake and waited. He waited until just before midnight. Then he crept out of bed and down the stairs.

Outside, it was pitch dark. Danny shone his torch ahead of him. He could just see a light at the bottom of the garden. Slowly, he made his way towards it. Now, he could hear that sound again. Chuff, chuff, chuff.

Danny reached the railway. In front of him was a row of gleaming black carriages. It was a train. Danny couldn't believe his eyes.

Chapter Three

Just then, Danny heard a man's voice.

"Hop on, son. We're late."

Danny couldn't see anyone, but a door opened in front of him.

Without thinking, he climbed on board. The train started moving. Danny reached for the door handle, but it was too late. Chuff, chuff, chuff. Faster and faster.

Danny blinked and looked around. A man dressed in a black uniform was coming towards him. He had a ticket machine.

"When to, son?" he asked, turning the handle of his ticket machine.

"When to?" Danny repeated in surprise. "Don't you mean where to?"

"No, son. This train will be calling at 1941, 1874 and 1600. Next stop, 1941. Is that all right for you?"

Danny nodded. The man gave him a ticket, then carried on along the carriage.

"When to?" The words rattled round in Danny's head. This must be some sort of time train. He was going back in time to 1941. But that was wartime, Danny thought. He had done the Second World War at school. He remembered looking at pictures of houses and factories built in grey London brick. Some had sandbags piled outside the doors. Others had crosses of sticky tape on the windows. That was how people tried to stop bombs blasting out the glass.

The train was slowing down. Now it stopped. Everyone started getting off. Danny followed the crowd through the station and down to the underground.

He would try to get to Piccadilly Circus. He had been there before. Then he would find a policeman and ask him what to do.

Chapter Four

People were hurrying into the underground.

"No room down there, son," someone said to him. "They're packed in like sardines."

Danny reached the bottom of the steps, but he couldn't go any further. The underground was full of people sleeping. They lay huddled under rugs and blankets. Some had suitcases with them. Babies were crying. The air was hot and smelly.

"Want to buy anything to eat?" a woman asked Danny. She was carrying a basket of buns and apples.

"No, thanks. I have to get to Piccadilly Circus," Danny said. He needed to get out into the fresh air.

Danny stepped out into the black night. He could hear voices and footsteps but it was too dark to see anything.

He turned on his torch and shone it ahead of him.

"Hey, turn that light out," someone shouted at him.

"But I can't see ..." Danny said.

"Don't you know there's a black-out?" the man asked crossly.

"Sorry," Danny said.

He had heard about the black-out. That was when people had to hang black curtains at their windows, so German bombers couldn't see the lights.

"Don't worry about the Warden," a voice in the dark said to Danny. The voice made Danny jump.

Chapter Five

It was a boy about Danny's age.

"Just follow the white lines. See?"

The boy pointed to white stripes painted along the pavement and around the lamp posts.

"Haven't you heard? They're even painting cows white, out in the country," the boy laughed. "There have been so many accidents because of the black-out, with the cars and that. You been bombed out?" he added. "Is that what they gave you to wear? Poor you!"

He looked Danny up and down. Danny thought he must look quite odd in his tracksuit and trainers.

"They've hit the docks tonight, see?" The boy pointed to a yellow glow in the sky. "A ship with a load of sugar was hit. There's sugar burning in the river. It's like treacle, they say." He put his hand out. "I'm Tom. What's your name?"

"Danny," said Danny.

Tom showed Danny a piece of twisted metal he was carrying under his arm.

"It's from a Dornier," he told him.

Danny gasped. Dorniers were German bomber planes. He had seen pictures of them.

“It came down a few streets from here. It’s from the tail, I think,” said Tom.

Danny ran his hand along the metal.

“Wow! A Dornier bomber! Can you find me one?” he asked Tom.

“We can try. Got to be careful, though. There’s already been one raid tonight, and there might be another,” Tom warned him.

Danny followed him along the street. They passed buildings with sandbags piled around the doors and boards nailed across the windows. Some of the shops had signs saying "Business as usual" and "No Looting".

Danny could see the beams of search lights lighting up the sky. Suddenly, there was a loud wailing sound.

"There goes the siren," Tom said. "Better get down to the shelter. Do you want to share our Anderson shelter? Mum won't mind."

Danny could hardly hear him now. Footsteps were clattering along the pavement as people hurried to find shelter. A menacing noise of aeroplane engines came from the sky. It sounded like millions of bees swarming together.

"Come on," Tom started running. "It's not far. That's our house, on the corner there."

Danny followed him, but in the dark he stumbled and dropped his torch.

"Hurry up, there!" someone shouted. The noise was louder now, the bees swarming overhead.

Chapter Six

Danny had lost sight of Tom, but he kept running, making for the house on the corner. He could hear the thud of anti-aircraft guns. Now there was a whistling sound, louder and louder.

Danny felt a huge crash, like the earth moving. He fell to the ground...

"You all right, son?" The Warden was standing over him. "You've had a lucky escape. They've had a direct hit over there."

"I was trying to get to Tom's house," Danny said. He scrambled to his feet. There was a strong smell of gas, and he could hear the sound of running water. "They've hit the mains," the Warden said. "The whole street. Look at it."

Danny stood in amazement. At the end of the street was Tom's house, the house on the corner. But the house had been sliced in two, like a giant birthday cake.

As torches flashed here and there, Danny could see pretty wallpaper on the walls and some pictures hanging crooked. Upstairs was part of a bedroom. He could see a brass bed and a row of hooks with coats hanging on them.

The Warden was helping people out of the Anderson shelters. Danny saw Tom among the others. He was standing with his mum and dad and his little brother. His dad had his arms around his family.

"Look, none of us is hurt," Tom's dad was saying. "That's the main thing."

"But look at our house!" Tom's mum wailed.

"Danny!" Tom shouted. "I thought you didn't make it."

Danny held his thumb up. "I'm all right! Are you?" he called back.

Tom was holding his brother's hand. "Yes," he said. "The shelter saved us."

"Come with me," Danny heard the Warden say. "We'll find you some clothes and blankets. Can't have you catching cold on top of everything!"

Just then, Danny heard a noise nearby. It was a dog barking. It was coming from a pile of bricks and wood. The dog was trapped.

"It's all right," Danny called. "I'll get you out."

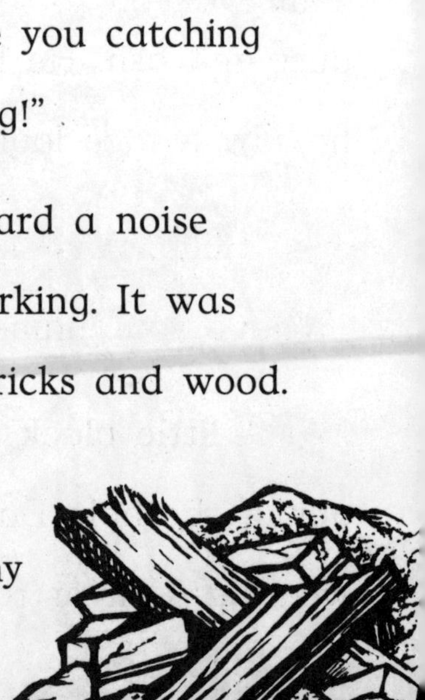

Chapter Seven

Danny got down on his knees and began moving bricks. The smoky air made him cough and his trainers were black with dust and ash. He had almost given up when he saw a face looking up at him.

"Hello, boy!" Danny said. "What's your name?"

A little black and white dog squeezed out of the hole Danny had made. He was wearing a silver tag round his neck with the name "Jester".

The dog barked and wagged his tail.

"Oh, Jester," Danny said. "I've got you out, but how do I get myself home?"

Jester barked again and ran ahead of Danny. He wanted Danny to follow him.

"All right, Jester," Danny said. "Lead on."

Jester led Danny along the street and down some steps. Every now and then he turned to see if Danny was following.

"Where are we going, Jester?" Danny asked.

He was beginning to feel tired. Then he saw the man in the black uniform with his ticket machine. He waved to Danny. He was about to blow a whistle. Jester had led him back to the Time Train.

Jester jumped on to the train and Danny followed him. The train started moving. Chuff, chuff, chuff. Faster and faster.

Danny sat with Jester on his lap. The sound of the train made him sleepy, and he closed his eyes.

When he opened them again, the train had stopped.

"All change," the ticket man was calling.

Chapter Eight

Danny stepped off the train. He looked for Jester, but he couldn't see him anywhere. There was the garden gate. He was back in his own garden and his own time.

Danny felt so tired he crept to bed and slept until morning. When he woke, he thought it must all have been a dream. Then he saw his trainers, black with dust and smoke. His torch was missing, too.

Danny ran out into the garden and down to the railway. Bees were buzzing round the tall weeds that covered the tracks.

Then Danny saw something moving in the nettles. It was a little black and white dog, with a silver tag around his neck. It was impossible, because he came from another time. But it was Jester.

"Jester!" Danny called. Jester heard him and began to wag his tail.

When to tonight? Danny wondered.